Of Gods and Evolution
An Alternate Theory

by

Mr. Lynn W. Grilley

DORRANCE
PUBLISHING CO
EST. 1920
PITTSBURGH, PENNSYLVANIA 15238

Dorrance Publishing Co
585 Alpha Drive
Pittsburgh, PA 15238
Visit our website at www.dorrancebookstore.com

ISBN: 979-8-89027-324-6
eISBN: 979-8-89027-822-7

Before I get started, I would like to thank all the websites and publications for their help in the research to aid me in developing my theory. Ancient Aliens and Unexplained Artifacts, Prehistoric Archaeology Site, and the BBC Ancient Aliens Site have many, many websites to get information from. The pictures I have included in this story are mostly all from the internet. I have decided to use text found on the internet as well and will use parentheses to indicate that these are quotes from people who have greater knowledge of the subject than I do.

"The first planet is a rocky, terrestrial planet. It has a solid and active surface with mountains, valleys, canyons, plains and so much more. It is special because it is an ocean planet. Water covers 70% of its surface."

"Its atmosphere is made mostly of nitrogen and has plenty of oxygen for us to breathe. The atmosphere also protects it from incoming meteoroids, most of which break up in its atmosphere before they can strike the surface as meteorites. It is the third planet from the Sun in our solar system."

"Even though Planet 2 isn't the closest planet to the Sun, it is still the hottest. It has a thick atmosphere full of the greenhouse gas carbon dioxide and clouds made of sulfuric acid. The gas traps heat and keeps it toasty warm. In fact, it's so hot on Planet 2, metals like lead would be puddles of melted liquid. It looks like a very active planet. It has mountains and volcanoes. It is similar in size to Planet 1."

"Planet 2 is unusual because it spins the opposite direction of Planet 1 and most other planets. And its rotation is very slow. It takes about 243 Earth days to spin around just once. Because it's so close to the Sun, a year goes by fast. It takes 225 Planet 1 days for Planet 2 to go all the way around the Sun."

"Planet 3 is the smallest planet in our solar system. It's just a little bigger than Planet 1's moon. It is the closest planet to the sun, but it's actually not the hottest. Planet 2 is hotter. Planet 3 is one of the rocky planets. It has a solid surface that is covered with craters. It has no atmosphere, and it doesn't have any moons. Planet 3 likes to keep things simple."

"This small planet spins around slowly compared to Planet 1, so one day lasts a long time. Planet 3 takes 59 Planet 1 days to make one full rotation. A year on Planet 3 goes by fast. Because it's the closest planet to the sun, it doesn't take very long to go all the way around. It completes one revolution around the sun in just 88 Planet 1 days. If you lived on Planet 3 you'd have a birthday every three months!"

"A day on Planet 3 is not like a day on Planet 1. The sun rises and sets each and every day. Because Planet 3 has a slow spin and short year, it takes a long time for the sun to rise and set there. Planet 3 only has one sunrise every 180 Earth days."

Most people would say that it is Earth, Venus, and Mercury that I am thinking about. However, what if it is several hundred million years ago or maybe billions of years ago? And the three planets are Mars, Earth, and Venus.

In the 1950s there were a few scientists who were hypothesizing that the sun was shrinking. Today, thanks to the Hubble Telescope, they are saying that the galaxies and universes are expanding. If the galaxies and universes are expanding, then it is logical to believe that the solar systems within those universes, including ours, are also expanding. This would mean that a few billion years ago Mars would be approximately the same distance from the sun as Earth is today.

"Earth's atmosphere is 78 percent nitrogen, 21 percent oxygen and 1 percent other ingredients—the perfect balance to breathe and live.

"The Earth's inner core is about the same temperature as the sun.

"According to radiometric dating estimation and other evidence, Earth formed over 4.5 billion years ago."

The reason I have highlighted the Earth's core temperature above is to note that it is as hot as the sun's temperature.

One of the major phenomena occurring on the sun is solar flares.

Solar flares are enormous explosions of energy that are released from the sun. It takes only a few minutes for these intense bursts of radiation to reach millions of degrees, and their effects can be devastating—causing blackouts and interfering with satellites.

"What are solar flares?"

Solar flares are essentially giant explosions on the surface of the sun, with the amount of energy that they release being equivalent to millions of nuclear bombs detonating simultaneously. These can last from minutes to hours, and are usually seen by scientists through x-rays and optical light."

"As Solar flares extend to the outer layer of the Sun, known as the corona, which consists of rarefied gas that reaches temperatures of up to 100 million degrees."

When a solar flare occurs, the common belief is that the energy is then drawn back into the sun by its gravitational pull. But what if during some of the more violent eruptions a small amount of energy escapes into space? After hundreds of millions of years or billions of years, the energy would start to collect together and start forming a new planet.

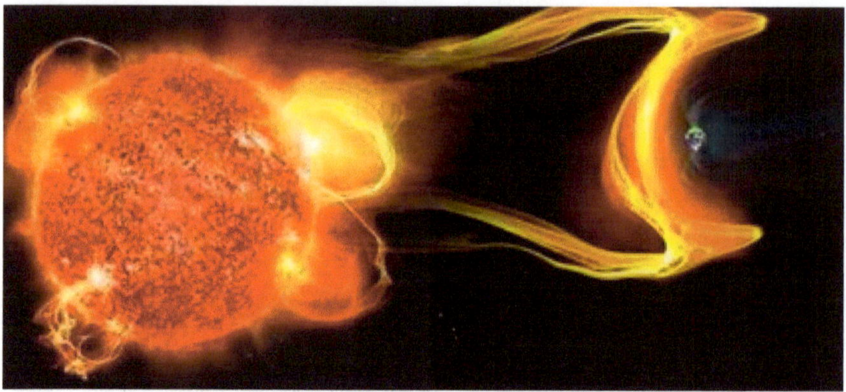

As the years pass, the new planet would start to develop an outer crust. Then an atmosphere. Eventually life of some form would start to appear.

The first forms of life would be microorganisms and then plant life. As plant life increased, the atmosphere would become more breathable. Then reptiles and other forms of life such as those now abundant on Earth would start to appear.

"Scientists at MIT, Cardiff University, and elsewhere have observed what may be signs of life in the clouds of our other, even closer planetary neighbor, Venus. While they have not found direct evidence of living organisms there, it must be some sort of 'aerial' life form in Venus' clouds—the only portion of what is otherwise a scorched and inhospitable world. Their discovery and analysis is published today in the journal *Nature Astronomy*."

"The astronomers, led by Jane Greaves of Cardiff University, detected in Venus' atmosphere a spectral fingerprint, or light-based signature, of phosphine. MIT scientists have previously shown that if this stinky, poisonous gas were ever detected on a rocky, terrestrial planet, it could only be produced by a living organism. The researchers made the detection using the James Clerk Maxwell telescope in Hawaii and the Atacama Large Millimeter Array observatory in Chile."

"The MIT team followed up the new observation with an exhaustive analysis to see whether anything other than life could have produced phosphine in Venus' harsh, sulfuric environment. Based on the many scenarios they considered the team concludes that there is no explanation for the phosphine detected in Venus' clouds, other than the presence of life."

"'It's very hard to prove a negative,' says Clara Sousa-Silva, research scientist in MIT's department of Earth, Atmospheric and Planetary Sciences (EAPS). 'Now, Astronomers will think of all the ways to justify phosphine without life, and I welcome that. Please do, because we are at the end of our possibilities to show abiotic processes that can make phosphine.'"

"'This means either this is life, or it's some sort of physical or chemical process that we do not expect to happen on rocky planets,' adds coauthor and EAPS Research Scientist Janusz Petkowski."

The most popular belief is that life cannot exist on Venus because the surface is too hot. However, we have life on certain areas of Earth that shouldn't be able to sustain life either. Two of the most interesting are shown below:

"Not too long ago, scientists studying the ocean made a fascinating discovery that has helped us better understand our planet Earth. Down in the deep and dark waters, they found hot springs on the ocean floor releasing warm and mineral-rich fluids—these are called hydrothermal vents."

"Hydrothermal vents are often associated with undersea volcanoes. This is because the vents are created and sustained by the heat of volcanic activity at tectonic plate boundaries, found throughout the globe."

"Despite the seemingly harsh volcanic environment these vents are actually home to a variety of life. Microbes, such as bacteria and archaea, live here—harvesting chemical energy from the hydrothermal fluid. These microbes form the base of a unique food chain that includes tube worms, shrimp, and even crabs that live in the communities around the vents."

"In 2010 a team of researchers, led by Felisa Wolfe-Simon, a microbiologist at the Lawrence Berkeley National Laboratory I California, published a remarkable paper in the (*Journal of Science*) in which they claimed to have discovered a bacterium that grew and metabolized using arsenic instead of phosphorus. At the same time as the paper, NASA put out a document entitled 'NASA-Funded-Funded Research Discovers Life Built with Toxic Chemical.'"

"This claim was met with immediate skepticism, bordering on outright derision, in the biology community. Most experts in microbiology poured scorn on the claim that organisms on Earth could use arsenic as a substitute for phosphorus, and, this criticism has been borne out by subsequent investigations."

"Although the bacterial species in question, GFAJ-1, is certainly highly tolerant of arsenic-rich environments, it turns out that, like all other terrestrial life it uses phosphorus—not arsenic—in its DNA. What Wolfe-Simon and her team had discovered was not arsenic based life but instead a microbial species of extremophiles that were able to tolerate high arsenic concentrations but still needed phosphorus to grow and divide."

So the correct response about whether life can exist on Venus would be, life as we know it can't.

There is evidence at several ancient sites on Earth that appear to show drawings or figurines of astronauts.

"Ancient astronauts (or ancients aliens) refers to a pseudoscientific hypothesis which holds that intelligent extraterrestial beings visited Earth and made contact with humans in antiquity and prehistoric times. Proponents suggest that this contact influenced the development of modern cultures, technologiess, religiond, and human biology.

"The idea that ancient astronauts existed and visited Earth is not taken seriously by academics and archaeologists, who consider it to be pseudo archaeological and/or unscientific. It has received no credible attention in peer reviewed studies. When proponents of the idea present evidence in favor of their beliefs, it is often distorted or fabricated."

Perhaps the best evidence of ancient aliens can be found in the ancient cave paintings around the world. Hundreds of unexplained images have been discovered on every continent, and many of these clearly represent alien creatures, alien spacecrafts, and other unexplained objects or out-of-place technology.

Cave painting

Strange suited figure found in Kiev. What appears to be a man wearing a helmet. It dates to ca. 4,000 B.C.

If early visitors came to Earth in spacesuits, then it would indicate that Earth's atmosphere was not breathable.

Many theories of aliens visiting Earth include they came from outer space. Please understand that I was a true *Star Trek* fan. But to believe that a large metallic object could travel through space at the speed of light or faster would, in the words of the late great actor Leonard Nimoy, be "highly illogical." However, travel between planets such as Mars to Earth or Earth to Venus would be possible. In fact, there have been several successful missions to both planets and more being planned.

I haven't read the Quran or any of the other religious stories on how the Earth and mankind came into existence. So I will talk about the one I do know about, and you can see if it comes close to how your religion believes it happened.

"The Book of Genesis opens the Bible with the story of creation. God, a spirit hovering over an empty, watery void, creates the world by speaking into the darkness and calling into being light, sky, land, vegetation, and living creatures over the course of six days. Each day, he pauses to pronounce his works 'good.' On the sixth day, God declares his intention to make a being in his 'own image,' and he creates humankind. He fashions a man out of dust and forms a woman out of the man's rib. God places the two people, Adam and Eve, in the idyllic garden of Eden, encouraging them to procreate and to enjoy the created world fully, and forbidding them to eat from the tree of the knowledge of good and evil."

"In the garden, Eve encounters a crafty serpent who convinces her to eat the tree's forbidden fruit, assuring her that she will not suffer if she does so. Eve shares the fruit with Adam, and the two are immediately filled with shame and remorse. While walking in the garden, God discovers their disobedience. After cursing the serpent, he turns and curses the couple. Eve, he says, will be cursed to suffer painful childbirth and must submit to her husband's authority. Adam is cursed to toil and work the ground for food. The two are subsequently banished from Eden.

"Sent out into the world, Adam and Eve give birth to two sons, Cain and Abel. Cain, a farmer, offers God a portion of his crops one day as a sacrifice, only to learn that God is more pleased when Abel, a herdsman, presents God with the fattest portion of his flocks. Enraged, Cain kills his brother. God exiles Cain from his home to wander in the land east of Eden. Adam and Eve give birth to a third son, Seth."

The story continues that Cain left Eden and found a wife. If Adam and Eve were the first man and woman on Earth, where did the woman that Cain married come from?

As noted earlier, the first visitors to Earth had what appeared to be spacesuits to provide oxygen. Was the Garden of Eden a biodome to provide oxygen and allow Adam and Eve to adjust to Earth's atmosphere? Were there other biodomes in the area? Had the natural evolution of mankind advanced to the point where Cain could find a wife? Were visitors from Mars now able to breathe the air on Earth without spacesuits? Or maybe a combination of all three scenarios?

There are many archaeological discoveries on Earth that suggest that beings of superior knowledge may have been here in the past. Not necessarily superior intelligence but superior knowledge. What is meant by this statement is that a doctor and an architect may have the same IQ, but the doctor would have the superior knowledge of medicine and the architect would have the superior knowledge of building design.

Teotihuacan: It is true—some ancient monuments demonstrate a thorough knowledge of astronomy surpassing knowledge of later cultures. The Pyramid of the Sun at Mexico's Teotihuacan lies at the center of a complex of pyramids, each aligned with a planet in the solar system. It is true—some ancient monuments demonstrate a thorough knowledge of astronomy surpassing knowledge of later cultures. The Pyramid of the Sun at Mexico's Teotihuacan lies at the center of a complex of pyramids, each aligned with a planet in the solar system.

The Nazca Lines

"Etched into a high plateau in Peru's Nazca Desert, a series of ancient designs stretching more than 50 miles has baffled archaeologists for decades. Along with simple lines and geometric shapes, they include drawings of animals, birds and humans, some measuring more than 600 feet across. Because of their colossal size, the figures can only be appreciated from way up in the air—and there is no evidence that the Nazca people, who inhabited the area between 300 B.C. and 800 A.D., invented flying machines. According to ancient alien theorists, the figures were used to guide spaceships as they came in for a landing, and the lines served as runways."

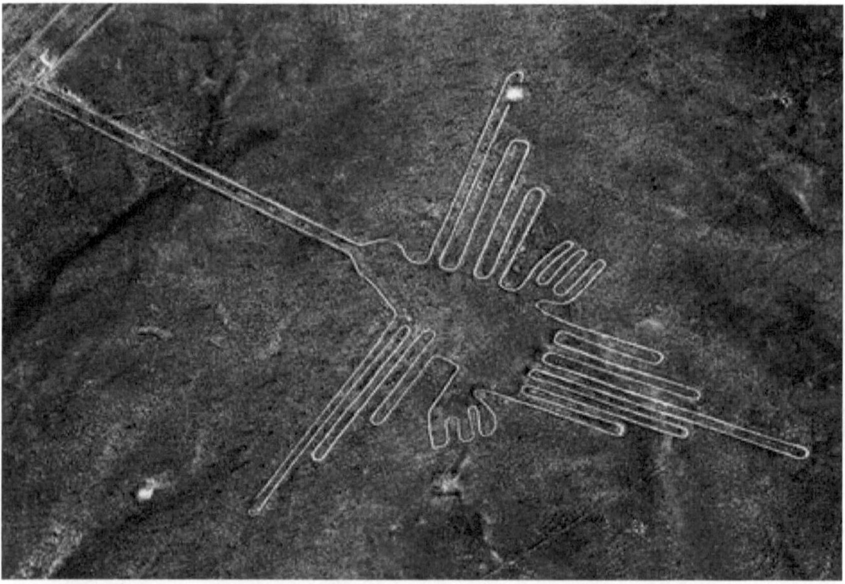

"A huge circle of stones, some weighing as much as 50 tons, sits in the English countryside outside Salisbury. Known as Stonehenge, the Neolithic monument inspired Swiss author Erich von Däniken to suggest it was a model of the solar system that also functioned as an alien landing pad—after all, how else could those massive stones have ended up hundreds of miles from their home quarry?

"No one knows what, exactly, the meaning of Stonehenge is, but, as with all the other sites in this collection, the explanation is not aliens. Instead, scientists have demonstrated it's, actually possible, to build such a thing using technologies that would have been around 5,000 years ago, when the earliest structures at the site were built.

"And now, it appears as though the stones are aligned with solstices and eclipses, suggesting the Stonehenge builders were at least keeping an eye on the heavens, even if they didn't come from above."

What Is the Mayan Civilization?

The Ancient Mayan people lived in Mesoamerica—depicted on the map.

Ancient Mayans refer to the civilization of people that lived and prospered in the tropical lowlands of Central America or present-day Guatemala.

Around 6000 B.C., the hunter-gatherers in Mesoamerica discovered techniques to domesticate plants; this was their first step to a sedentary lifestyle.

Effective agricultural methods resulted in the formation of several cities and villages across modern-day North Mexico throughout Central America. This region is known as the Mesoamerican cultural area.

Mesoamerica was the birthing ground of several cultures that are now broadly known as the Maya Civilization. The people of Mesoamerica held various identities and spoke various languages. They were not united by any one political entity.

They excelled in agriculture, architecture, math, calendar, and astronomical systems. Their most noteworthy achievement is the Maya glyphs, a writing system that included logograms and syllabic symbols.

Maya Civilization is one of the most important civilizations in human history. It is one of the earliest civilizations to have used the number zero.

In the 15th century, due to the Spanish invasion in Mexico and Central America, the Maya Civilization was taken over and many of the artifacts and literature were destroyed.

There are over six million Maya people who still live in Central America. Most of them speak Spanish and one of the 28 surviving Maya languages.

"The Mayan Empire, centered in the tropical lowlands of what is now Guatemala, reached the peak of its power and influence around the sixth century A.D. The Maya excelled at agriculture, pottery, writing, calendars and mathematics, and left behind an astonishing amount of impressive architecture and symbolic artwork. Most of the great stone cities of the Maya were abandoned by A.D. 900, however, and since the 19th century scholars have debated what might have caused this dramatic decline."

"Did you know? Among the earliest Maya a single language existed, but by the Preclassic Period a great linguistic diversity developed among the various Maya peoples. In modern-day Mexico and Central America, around 5 million people speak some 70 Maya languages; most of them are bilingual in Spanish."

"Within that expanse, the Maya lived in three separate sub-areas with distinct environmental and cultural differences: the northern Maya lowlands on the Yucatan Peninsula; the southern lowlands in the Peten district of northern Guatemala and adjacent portions of Mexico, Belize and western

Honduras; and the southern Maya highlands, in the mountainous region of southern Guatemala.”

“Most famously, the Maya of the southern lowland region reached their peak during the Classic Period of Maya civilization (A.D. 250 to 900), and built the great stone cities and monuments that have fascinated explorers and scholars of the region to this day.”

Athens was an ancient Greek city.

“Ancient Greek civilization, the period between the end of the Mycenaean civilization (1200 B.C.) and the death of Alexander the Great” (323 B.C.) that significantly influenced later Western culture in politics, philosophy, and art.”

“Little is known about the earliest period of ancient Greek civilization, and many extant writings pertain only to life in Athens. Ancient Greece at its height comprised settlements in Asia Minor, southern Italy, Sicily, and the Greek islands. It was divided into city-states—Athens and Sparta were among the most powerful—that functioned independently of one another. There were frequent wars between Athens, Sparta, and their allies, including the Peloponnesian War (431–404 B.C.) and later the Corinthian War (395–386 B.C.).”

"Some city-states, including Athens, were governed by an early system of democracy that served as a precursor for later systems of government in the Western world. An interest in athletic competition was prevalent in ancient Greek culture, and the first Olympic Games were held in 776 B.C."

"Ancient Greek culture continued on in the writings of its philosophers, notably Plato and Aristotle; its historians, notably Thucydides; and in the literature of Homer, the presumed author of *The Iliad* and *The Odyssey*."

"The ancient Greeks also contributed to developments in art and architecture through the numerous sculptures and temples they constructed—the buildings of the Athenian acropolis, for example—to memorialize their deities."

"Ancient Egypt can be thought of as an oasis in the desert of northeastern Africa, dependent on the annual inundation of the Nile River to support its agricultural population. The country's chief wealth came from the fertile floodplain of the Nile valley, where the river flows between bands of limestone hills, and the Nile delta, in which it fans into several branches north of present-day Cairo."

In urban and elite contexts, the Egyptian ideal was the nuclear family, but on the land and even within the central ruling group there is evidence for extended families. Egyptians were monogamous, and the choice of partners in marriage, for which no formal ceremony or legal sanction is known, did not follow a set pattern. Consanguineous marriage was not practiced during the Dynastic period, except for the occasional marriage of a brother and sister within the royal family, and that practice may have been open only to kings or heirs to the throne. Divorce was in theory easy, but it was costly. Women had a legal status only marginally inferior to that of men. They could own and dispose of property in their own right, and they could initiate divorce and other legal proceedings. They hardly ever held administrative office but increasingly were involved in religious cults as priestesses or "chantresses." Married women held the title "mistress of the house," the precise significance of which is unknown. Lower down the social scale, they probably worked on the land as well as in the house.

The uneven distribution of wealth, labor, and technology was related to the only partly urban character of society, especially in the 3rd millennium B.C.E. The country's resources were not fed into numerous provincial towns but instead were concentrated to great effect around the capital—itself a dispersed string of settlements rather than a city—and focused on the central figure in society, the king. In the 3rd and early 2nd millennia, the elite ideal, expressed in the decoration of private tombs, was manorial and rural. Not until much later did Egyptians develop a more pronouncedly urban character.

"In cosmogonical terms, Egyptian society consisted of a descending hierarchy of the gods, the king, the blessed dead, and humanity (by which was understood chiefly the Egyptians). Of these groups, only the king was single, and hence he was individually more prominent than any of the others. A text that summarizes the king's role states that he 'is on earth for ever and ever,' judging mankind and propitiating the gods, and setting order in place of disorder. He gives offerings to the gods and mortuary offerings to the spirits [the blessed dead]."

The king was imbued with divine essence but not in any simple or unqualified sense. His divinity accrued to him from his office and was reaffirmed through rituals, but it was vastly inferior to that of major gods; he was god rather than man by virtue of his potential, which was immeasurably greater than that of any human being. To humanity, he manifested the gods on Earth, a conception that was elaborated in a complex web of metaphor and doctrine; less directly, he represented humanity to the gods. The text quoted above also gives great prominence to the dead, who were the object of a cult for the living and who could intervene in human affairs; in many periods the chief visible expenditure and focus of display of nonroyal individuals, as of the king, was on provision for the tomb and the next world.

Chinese, Mayan, and Egyptian artifacts seem to show what appears to be airplanes. I have included a few images below.

In one of BBC's ancient alien television shows, they said that they made a model of a similar of one of these artifacts, put a motor and a propeller on it, and it flew. This would seem to indicate that ancient civilizations were aware of flying machines.

The Megalithic Baalbek Temple: An Ancient "Landing Place"?

"When one considers the mysteries of ancient megalithic ruins, famous sites such as Stonehenge, Palenque, and Göbekli Tepe come to mind, though less often are the temple grounds of Baalbek mentioned in the same breath. There, perched 3,000 feet atop a sacred hill in Lebanon's Beqaa Valley, lay the ruins of one of the world's most massive megalithic sites, containing some of the heaviest quarried stones of antiquity. Still, little is understood of its construction.

"Baalbek is located in the northeast of Lebanon, about 60 miles outside of Beirut, making it a difficult place to travel these days. But during the time of Roman imperialism, it was known as Heliopolis, the 'City of the Sun,' founded by Alexander the Great in 334 B.C. Baalbek became the site of Roman temples dedicated to Jupiter, Bacchus, and Venus, based on a popular cult devoted to this famous triumvirate."

"Though the foundational stones and the location in which they were quarried have been known for some time, the site's biggest megalith was discovered just recently. Weighing in at a whopping 1,620 tons, it outweighs another mysteriously gargantuan monolith from the same quarry, known as the Pregnant Mother Stone, by 400 tons."

"Moving the trilithon into place today would require the effort of some of the world's most powerful cranes, yet in the time of its alleged construction, the stones were somehow situated through primitive means so precisely, that one has difficulty slipping a sheet of paper between them today."

"To put the sheer weight of these stones into perspective, one might compare them to the stones used to construct Stonehenge, which weighs in at around 25 tons each—a fraction of the trilithon stones' weight."

"Researchers including Graham Hancock, find this difficult to comprehend, leading him to believe in the possibility that an antediluvian, or pre-flood, civilization with advanced technology may have been responsible for the trilithon, upon which the Romans later constructed their temple. In fact, Hancock says he believes the trilithon may be 12,000 or more years old, predating Roman construction by around 10,000 years."

If all of these ancient civilizations existed and were able to accomplish these amazing constructions and understood astrology and knew about flight, what happened to all of them? Did they die of starvation, did they die because of diseases, or just moved away?

To show one thing that may have happened, I will go to the Bible again. Please see if your religion has a similar belief about what I am suggesting. One thing that many of the ancient sites have in common is flooding.

"In the Judeo-Christian flood story, God became angry with the sins of mankind. He told his faithful servant, Noah, to build an ark large enough for his family (which included eight people; his wife, his three sons and their wives) and two of every creature on earth. God delivered the promised deluge, killing everyone and everything on earth except the population of the ark."

"After the flood, the ark came to rest on a mountain top, a detail that is repeated in many stories across different cultures. This was an attempt to show the immense depth of the water, that it was higher than the mountains. Noah and his family were the only humans alive and are presumably the origins of the current human race."

"The same narrative is mirrored in the Quran: Allah told Noah to build the ark, the flood came, and then from Noah, the world began again."

"South America: In Inca mythology, Unu Pachakuti is the name of a flood that Viracocha caused to destroy the people around Lake Titicaca, saving two to bring civilization to the rest of the world."

"The Inca's supreme being and creator god, Con Tici (Kon Tiki) Viracocha, first created a race of giants, but they were unruly, so he destroyed them in a mighty flood and turned them to stone. Following the deluge, he created human beings from smaller stones. In other versions of this story, the impious race is the pre-Inca civilization of the Tiahuanaco Americans about Lake Titicaca, the large high lake in the Andes. Viracocha drowns them and spares two, a man and a woman, to start the human race anew. Some versions of the Unu Pachakuti have the surviving man and woman floating to Lake Titicaca in a wooden box."

"Philippines: One year, when the rainy season should have come, it did not. When the river dried up, the people dug into its grave, hoping to find the soul of the river. They struck a great spring, which angered the river gods. It began to rain and the river overflowed its banks. The resulting flood wiped out all of humanity save for two survivors, Wigan and Bugan, who repopulated the earth once the waters receded."

"Greek: Plato makes reference to great floods in several of his dialogues, including Timaeus, Critias, and Laws. In Timaeus (22) and in Critias (111–112) he describes the 'great deluge of all,' specifying the one survived by Deucalion and Pyrrha, as having been preceded by 9,000 years of history before the time of Solon, during the 10th millennium BCE. In Laws, Book III,[2] argues that a great flood had occurred ten thousand years [before his time], as opposed to only 'one or two thousand years that have elapsed' since the discovery of music, and other inventions. Plato also alludes to a well-known event of great destruction, in Statesman (270), where 'only a small part of the human race survives,' presumably also referring to the flood of Deucalion."

In both the Bible and the Quran, Noah was warned in advance of a great flood. Flooding can occur in many ways. Heavy rains for many days, underwater earthquakes, and underwater volcanic eruptions. All of these scenarios would be very difficult to predict in advance.

Because astrology was known in ancient times, there is one way that widespread flooding could be predicted in advance. Suppose a massive meteor landed in a large body of water. Maybe not as big as the one that scientists say wiped out the dinosaurs, but maybe as large as the following meteors below.

"The Beaverhead impact structure is the 2nd largest impact structure within the U.S. It lies within the states of Idaho and Montana. Estimated at 60 kilometers (37 mi) in diameter, it is the 9th largest impact crater on Earth.

"The third largest asteroid impact caused the formation of Acraman Crater with a radius of 55.9234 miles (90 km) in the Gawler Ranges, South Australia, Australia, 580 million years ago. Its location is marked by Lake Acraman, a playa lake or lake whose bottom has dried up due to large evaporation."

If a meteor of that size landed in an ocean, two things would happen. First, a huge tidal wave (or tsunami, if you prefer) would move away from the entry point in a 360° direction. Secondly hundreds of gallons of water, maybe even millions of gallons, would be vaporized into the atmosphere to fall back to Earth as rain. Because the moisture would be hot, it might rain for several days and nights. This would also explain why the flooding is both at sea level and in high mountain areas such as the Andes.

One thing that is hard to explain is, if ancient aliens had the ability to build and make these wonderful cities and large structures, why isn't there evidence of the tools they used to do it? The only logical reason I can think of is hundreds of thousands of years of earthquakes, volcanic eruptions, floods, geological upheavals, and meteor bombardments.

Does all of what I have talked about so far mean that I don't believe in God? No, it doesn't. In fact, it would appear that God, or Allah, or Buddha, or Odin, or whichever name you choose to use, may be a more powerful Entity than any of the religions give It, or He, or She credit for. Able to control the destiny of an entire solar system instead of one planet within that system.

Please understand that I don't have proof that any of my theory is correct. As of this moment in time, my theory is just that, a theory. In 1905, when Albert Einstein put forth his Theory of Relativity, his theory was also just a theory.

"Albert Einstein is easily one of the most brilliant physicists who ever lived. His theories of general relativity changed our understanding of the cosmos, as did his work on quantum theory. But his genius has also led many to hold him up as a poor stereotype of science. The lone genius who ignores the science of his day to overturn everything with a simple brilliant theory. He's become the icon of every crackpot who feels compelled to send emails to scientists about their ideas that will revolutionize science if we only take the time to listen (and work out all the math for them). But as revolutionary as Einstein's ideas were, they weren't entirely unexpected. Other scientists had similar ideas, and developed similar equations. Take, for example, Einstein's most famous equation, $E = mc2$."

"The equation appears in Einstein's 1905 paper 'Does the Inertia of a Body Depend Upon Its Energy Content?' and it expresses a fundamental connection between matter and energy. Energy was long known to be a property of matter in terms of its kinetic motion, heat and interactions, but Einstein's equation proposed that matter, simply by having mass, has an inherent amount of energy. It allowed us to understand how radioactive particles decay and how stars create energy through nuclear fusion."

"On April 14, 1932, the English physicist Sir John Douglas Cockcroft and the Irish physicist Ernest Walton split the atom for the first time using the nuclear particle accelerator they built, also the first particle accelerator in history."

Once the scientists split the atom, Einstein's theory became fact. So to determine if my theory or any part of it has any merit whatsoever, it will take the combined efforts of scientists, astrologists, archaeologists, geologists, religious scholars and, of course, time. There is one statement I can make about my theory that has a chance of being truthful, however. That would be, **if!** my theory is correct, then the next inhabitable in our solar system will be Venus, not Mars.

I would like to conclude my theory with a simple prayer.

May whichever God or Entity you believe in or personnel belief you have keep you safe and in good health.